THE AMAZING CAPTAIN CONCORDE

By day he is Paul Cookson – poet, performer and editor. By night he is Paul Cookson – husband and father. But in poetry performances he often transforms into *The Amazing Captain Concorde* (thanks to a pair of big red underpants and a plastic nose)! Paul has been doing this for over ten years – with the same pair of pants.

Paul is not a superhero really, although he did want to be Batman when he was younger. He lives in Retford, with his wife Sally and two children, Sam and Daisy.

David Parkins has illustrated numerous books, ranging from maths textbooks to *The Beano*. His picture books have been shortlisted for the Smarties Book Prize and the Kurt Maschler Award; and commended twice in the National Art Library Illustration Awards. He lives in Canada.

To Robin
Best wishes
Paul Cole

THE AMAZING CAPTAIN CONCORDE

Superhero Poems chosen by
PAUL COOKSON

Illustrated by David Parkins

MACMILLAN CHILDREN'S BOOKS

*Dedicated to all the staff at the Special Care Baby Unit,
Bassetlaw District Hospital. Real Superheroes, every one.*

First published 2000 as *Superheroes* by Macmillan Children's Books

This edition published 2011 by Macmillan Children's Books
a division of Macmillan Publishers Limited
20 New Wharf Road, London N1 9RR
Basingstoke and Oxford
Associated companies throughout the world
www.panmacmillan.com

ISBN 978-1-4472-0172-4 (TRADE)
ISBN 978-0-330-54591-4 (SPL)

1 3 5 7 9 8 6 4 2

A CIP catalogue record for this book is available from the British Library.

Printed and bound in the UK by CPI Mackays, Chatham ME5 8TD

'It's POETRYMAN!' by David Horner first published in *Phwoarr*
by Apple Pie Publications 2000.
'School Gate Protector' by Stewart Henderson first published in
Who Left Grandad at the Chip Shop? by Lion 2000.

Contents

Batman

Batman
Age 10½
Patrols the streets of his suburb
At night
Between 7 and 8 o'clock.
If he is out later than this
He is spanked
And sent to bed
Without supper.

Batman
Almost 11
Patrols the streets of his suburb
At night
If he has finished his homework.

Batman,
His secret identity
And freckles
Protected
By the mask and cloak
His Auntie Elsie
Made on her sewing machine,
Patrols
At night
Righting Wrongs.

Tonight he is on the trail of
Raymond age 11
(Large for his age)
Who has stolen Stephen's
Gobstoppers and football cards.

Batman
Patrolling the streets of his suburb
Righting Wrongs
Finds Raymond,
Demands the return of the stolen goods.
Raymond knocks him over,
Rips his mask,
Tears his cloak,
And steals his utility belt.
Batman starts to cry,
Wipes his eyes with his cape
(His hankie was in the belt).

Next day
Auntie Elsie says
This is the fourteenth time
I've had to mend your
Batman costume.
If it happens again
You'll have to whistle for it.

Batman
Eats a bag of crisps.

John Turner

Superhero's Diary

MONDAY
Turned back alien invasion fleet attacking planet Mars

TUESDAY
Tried out my latest powered boots by going round the stars

WEDNESDAY
Held up collapsing building after severe earthquake

THURSDAY
Retrieved a nuclear missile fired by mistake

FRIDAY
Kept afloat a sinking ship till safely on the shore

SATURDAY
Planned with other heroes to stop war for ever more

SUNDAY
Hit my thumb with hammer while repairing garden shed;
Made me feel all faint and funny; spent the afternoon in
bed.

Alan Priestley

Wherezebeen and Lazyboy

When the crime has been committed
And the police have been and gone
Wherezebeen and Lazyboy
Get their costumes on.

When the police have done their duty
and the crime is all wrapped up
Wherezebeen and Lazyboy
make some tea and drink a cup.

When the criminal is captured
and the police go home at ten past five
Wherezebeen and Lazyboy
finally arrive.

'Where's the police gone, Lazyboy?'
'Wherezebeen, where is the crime?'
Wherezebeen and Lazyboy
Wander homewards, take their time.

Ian McMillan

The Dynamic Chewo

The dynamic chewo tackle a formidable feast

DRIBBLE   BITE   CRUNCH

SMACK   CHEW

                                                MUNCH

SLOBBER   CHOMP

                                           SLURP

GNASH   LICK   BURP!

Supperheroes!

Philip Waddell

The Young Superheroes' School Trip

Supergirl
Wouldn't pay for her coach seat
Because she thought
It would be more fun to
Fly there
Instead.

Spiderboy
Climbed up the castle wall
And scared
Three Belgian tourists
So much that
They dropped their cameras.

Batgirl
Spent the whole day
Sulking
Behind her mask.

Conan the Warrior Boy
Picked a fight
With some kids
From another school.

The head teacher said –
Just because you've got superpowers
Doesn't mean
You can flout the rules.

Now they're all banned
From school trips
For the rest of the year

And they're in detention

Where the teacher
Pretends not to notice
The chess game which
Supergirl and Spiderboy
Are playing
On the ceiling . . .

John Turner

The Greatest of Them All

You can keep your superheroes
Like Batman and the rest –
I know a fella down our street
Who's easily the best!

He tears up toilet tissues,
He can break a twig in two,
He can lift a bag of feathers,
No, there's nothing he can't do.

He can bend a piece of cardboard,
He can frighten new-born flies,
And at snapping off a daisy head
He always takes first prize.

He's stronger than a sparrow
And he's faster than a snail,
He can punch a hole in newspapers
And never ever fail.

He's thinner than a matchstick
And his biceps look like peas,
His legs are like a spider's
And he's got two knobbly knees.

He's a legend in his lifetime
He's a hero through and through.
And who's this mighty little weed?
It's Superwimp – that's who!

Clive Webster

Mrs Superhero

All day,
he just sits there
reading next door's paper
with his X-ray vision.

Or he's off down the pub
with his super mates,
discussing world crises,
like should he wear a green cape?

Or flying off
to save the world,
from some deranged psychopath.

And he says he has to do it,
because he's got the powers
and the costume, and nobody else
could save the world like he does.

And he is good at it,
the superheroing,
but get him to wash the dishes?
Forget it!

John Davies

Interview with Mr Crabman, Superhero

May I sidle up to you
to ask a few questions?
> *Nothing too direct, please.*
Life cannot have been easy for you.
> *No, I had to claw my way to the top.*
You have a family.
> *A couple of nippers.*
You deal with specific crimes.
> *Mainly smash and crab.*
Do you stalk your prey?
> *These eyes were made for stalking.*
Tactics?
> *Pincer movements.*
How do you cope with injury?
> *I use crab sticks.*
How about transport?
> *I often call a taxicrab.*
Do clients pay up?
> *Most shell out at once.*
Do you have any support?
> *Yes, we have an annual crab meet.*
What happens?
> *We play crabble
> and sing our song –
> 'I did it sideways'.*

John C. Desmond

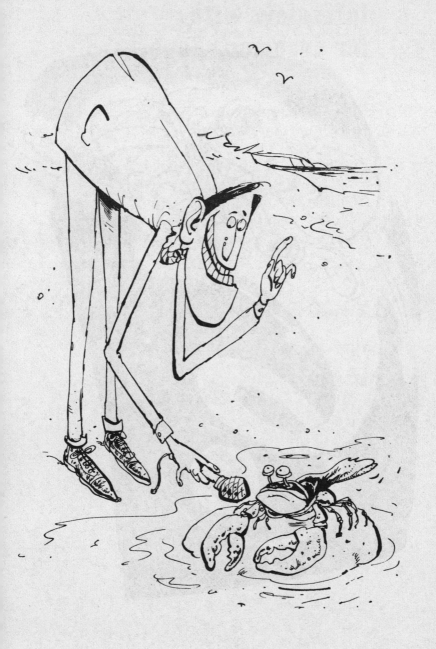

SuperSid's Shopping List

I was blasting off to Outer Space
When my mother said to me,
*Bring us back some Martian jam
And some Cassiopean tea,*

*And fetch a slab of the mint cake
They make on Venus Five,
And a quarter of Neptune fruit gums
For your little brother Clive,*

*And don't forget those pizzas
From the Western side of Saturn,
The ones with cute little purple spots
In super-galactic patterns –*

*You know, the ones our Sharon loves,
And don't forget your gran's
Red Plutonian cough drops,
And those things for scrubbing pans*

*They sell in the markets of Uranus
Made from the thickest bristle
Of green Uranian badgers,
The ones they train to whistle . . .*

And as I was flying out of range
I heard her shout . . .

> *Don't*
> > *forget,*
> > > *bring*
> > > > *back*
> > > > > *the*
> > > > > > *change!*

Matt Simpson

17

Goldilox Girl

Through the three bears' cottage
in a whirl
Yellow hair flowing:
Goldilox Girl!

Eat up your porridge,
do a twirl
break the chair,
Goldilox Girl!

Through the woods
doing good
helping Little Red Riding Hood!

No time to settle
feel her metal
cutting through the cage to Hansel and Gretel!

She's diamond
She's a pearl
Fairy tale heroine
Goldilox Girl!

Ian McMillan

Unmasked

Superheroes don't wear cardigans when it's cold
Superheroes don't wear cardigans when they're told

And as the temperature drops
to zero
and below,
Will he put on a scarf?
A superhero –
No.
Thick socks,
A winter coat,
A bobble hat?
None of that.

Just a pair of tights,
Boots,
Underpants,
And a thermal vest
To cover his chest.

But the mask?
Don't ask
Why?
Some say it's to hide his identity
But I think it's
To keep his nose warm.

Who's ever heard of a red-nosed superhero?

John Coldwell

School Gate Protector

There's a being who's bewitching,
she's also short and stout.
Her face is stern with sorcery
and twice a day she's out

to guard the zebra crossing
and halt traffic with a glare.
All juggernauts are powerless
at her piercing, peak-capped stare.

At rush hour she is ominous
for everyone must wait
and even red Ferraris
dare not accelerate.

Police cars, buses, cyclists
all quiver in the road
and woe betide the scuffed, white van
with crammed, uneven load.

All vehicles brake to worship her
they dip their lights half-beam
yet still her shapeless mac shines out,
a sort of grubby cream.

For the secret of her mighty rule
is a spindly, spellbound prop.
It's her magic wand of yellow –
a metal lollipop.

Stewart Henderson

Superman's Washing

'My tights have shrunk,' howled Superman.
'My pants have stretched and spread.
My super S has shrivelled
and my cape's now pink, not red.
I know she thinks I'm wonderful
But I shan't let Lois Lane,
no matter how she begs me,
wash my super clothes again.'

Marian Swinger

Batman Comes Undone!

Help! Disaster! Fire and smoke!
Robin's trod on Batman's cloak –
made a rip right up his back.
He'll have to wear his anorak.

Kate Williams

Metalman

I've got
>> Nerves of steel
>> An iron will
>> I'm as hard as nails
>> Invincible!

You can call me *Metalman*

Well no
>> I don't catch robbers
>> I don't stop crime
>> I get so weary
>> I have to take my time

OK, you can call me *Metal (fatigue) man*

So you
>> Won't catch me flying
>> I weigh a ton
>> Instead of running
>> I lumber along

Yes, you can call me *Heavy Metalman*

But I've got
>> Eyes that shine
>> A love that's strong
>> A heart of gold
>> A silver tongue

My girlfriend calls me *Precious*

But you'd better call me *Metalman*.

Bernard Young

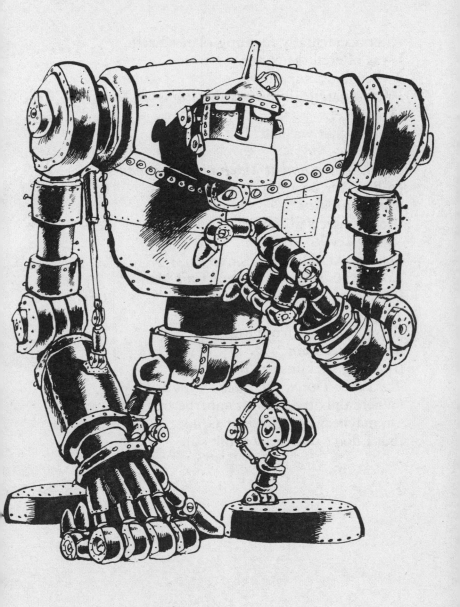

Superheroes I Could Have Been

After accidentally rescuing planet Earth,
I was offered the chance
To become a superhero.
Unfortunately all the best positions
Had gone.
This is what was left.

Liquid Refreshment Machine Repairman
(A lifesaver on a hot day)
Mosquito Man
(Keeps insects at bay)
Salting Icy Roads Man
(Saving skidding lorries and cars)
Confectionery Refreshment Unit Man
(Saving melting chocolate bars)
Tadpole Man
(Rescuing frogs from logs)
Stick Insect Man
(rescuing stick insects from frogs)
Ten Pence Down the Back of the Sofa Man
(Where only the bravest superheroes go)
Or, maybe *Super Zimmer Gran*
(but I don't somehow think so).

I could have been *Captain Decisive*
But I couldn't make up my mind
I could have been *Captain King of the Hill*
But I didn't feel so inclined
I could have been *Captain Upholsterer*
But I'd never have recovered
I could have been *Captain Apathy*
But I just couldn't be bothered.

Roger Stevens

It's POETRYMAN!

Who's got more go than a bowl of bran?
Look everybody, it's Poetryman!
Whose poems are always spick and span?
Look everybody, it's Poetryman!
Who's no rhyming also-ran?
Look everybody, it's Poetryman!
Whose lines nearly almost always sort of scan?
Look everybody, it's Poetryman!

1 2 3 4 – watch him mix a metaphor.

Whose verses fizz like Coke from a can?
Look everybody, it's Poetryman!
Whose choruses crackle like eggs in a pan?
Look everybody, it's Poetryman!
Whose smiles are sharp as suits from Milan?
Look everybody, it's Poetryman!
And Shakespeare says that he's a fan.
Look everybody, it's Poetryman!

2 4 6 8 – now see him alliterate.

From Alaska to Afghanistan –
  Look everybody, it's Poetryman!
There is no one better than –
  Look everybody, it's Poetryman!
Who's like a cross between Desperate Dan –
  Look everybody, it's Poetryman!
And an underfed orang-utan?
  Look everybody, it's Poetryman!

  3 5 7 9 – think he just ran out of rhyme . . .

  David Horner

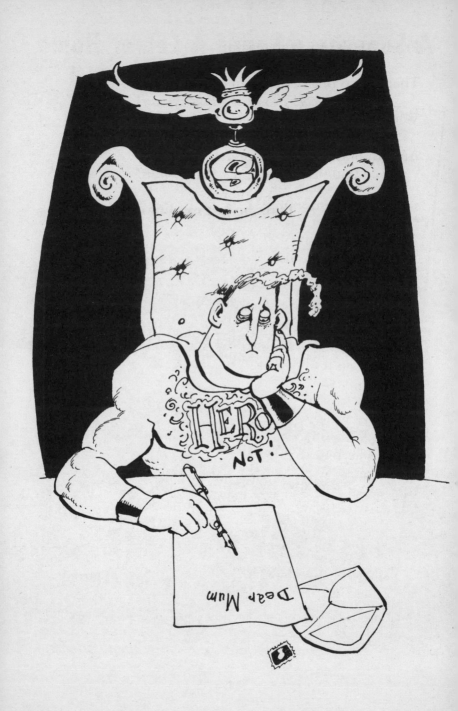

A Superhero Sends A Letter Home

Dear Mum,

Things haven't been too good just lately
Speeding bullets overtake me.
My dizzy spells and fear of heights
Inconvenience all my flights.
The purple tights you sent at last
Have given me a nasty rash.
X-ray vision's not all it seems
I'm sick of seeing bones and spleens.
My tinnitus is getting worse
The seams upon my trunks have burst.
I've got an aching in my head
I'm out of breath getting out of bed.
To top it all the yoghurt stains
In my satin cloak remain.
My love life hit a downward whirl
I'm no longer seeing Dandruff Girl.
She's gone off with Ali Tosis
The Bad Breath Boy who smells the
mostest.
I'm scared of going out at night
I run away when I should fight.
So as you see things could be better
But not much worse as I end this letter.
My super powers are minus zero
Your loving son,

A failing Hero
xxxx

Paul Cookson

Watch it!

Listen to me!
Yeah – me.
I know I'm small.
All right, I'm tiny
But I'm strong.
I've got special powers.
Extraordinary, scary powers –
And I'm warning you,
Don't mess with me.
Don't laugh.
Don't snigger.
Don't sneer.
Don't bring that cat
Anywhere near.
I won't tell you again.
I'm giving you
One last chance.
All right.
You asked for it.
!!NIP!!
I told you.
Don't mess with
SUPERSHREW!!

Trevor Millum

SITUATION VACANT

COULD YOU BE
**our next trainee
Superhero / heroine?**

Immediate vacancy exists for this challenging post
With excitement and adventure guaranteed uppermost.
Your duty will be to save the planet Earth
From an evil and imminent alien invasion.
Starting salary by negotiation.
Expected age range from twenty through to forty.
Applicants should be fit and keen and sporty.
Ability to fly (without wings) even better.
Apply now, by letter,
With full details and C.V.
To:
Save the World plc,
P.O. Box 303,
Gotham City,
U.S.A.
(Closing date for applications is 31st May)

Alan Priestley

Excuses Girl

Ten past nine and you're still in the sweet shop
school began some time ago
now you're facing a huge detention
not to mention the awkward fact
that you haven't finished last night's homework
or the one from the night before.

Excuses Girl will put things right
Excuses Girl brings everything you need
Excuses Girl blows away your problems
Excuses Girl gets you believed.

No PE kit?
Your shorts and T-shirt were eaten by a giant purple
rabbit.
Messy school work?
Tiny aliens tap-danced all night with wet feet on your
books.
Late for assembly?
You took the short cut by way of Alaska.
Didn't practise your guitar?
You were too busy last night giving a tuba recital at the
Albert Hall.
Talking in assembly?
You were secretly communicating with MI5 down your
electronic socks.
Got your spellings wrong?
This is really The Magic Language of the Incas, spells
not spellings. Beware!

Need to leave early?
She's at the classroom door looking like your Gran.
Didn't do your homework?
She'll write a note in your mum's writing saying you had
24-hour chicken pox.
Unfortunately
the paper aeroplane you threw at the head teacher
looped the loop and whizzed up his hairy nostril.
Sorry! You're for it. Excuses Girl can't solve every problem.

David Harmer

Lonely Hearts

Superheroine –
        nine feet high [with own cape]
        wishes to meet
        Supermanhero –
for outings to:
        burning buildings
        haunted castles
        snake pits
        and sinking ships.

Also: foreign travel – Mars, Mercury, Jupiter etc.

MUST like: clubs (karate)
        clothes (combat)
        bombs (unexploded)

and car driving – preferably off cliffs.

Also: pets – piranhas, sharks, poisonous reptiles.

Please include photo. (no masks)

Peter Dixon

The Amazing Captain Concorde

IS IT A BIRD?
IS IT A PLANE?
LOOK AT THE SIZE OF THE NOSE ON HIS FACE!
IS IT A BIRD?
IS IT A PLANE?
CAPTAIN CONCORDE IS HIS NAME!
CAPTAIN CONCORDE NEEEEOOWN!
CAPTAIN CONCORDE NEEEEOOWN!

A man with a mission
Radar vision
A nose that's supersonic
Faster than the speed of sound
His Y-fronts are bionic
Big and baggy
Red and saggy
Streamlined underpants
Always ready
Hi-tech sheddies
Crooks don't stand a chance.

IS IT A BIRD?
IS IT A PLANE?
LOOK AT THE SIZE OF THE NOSE ON HIS FACE!
IS IT A BIRD?
IS IT A PLANE?
CAPTAIN CONCORDE IS HIS NAME!
CAPTAIN CONCORDE NEEEEOOWN!
CAPTAIN CONCORDE NEEEEOOWN!

Anytime anyplace anywhere
But never ever Mondays
Coz that's the day the Captain's mum
Washes his red undies

Anytime anyplace anywhere
His power is fantastic
Everything's under control
With super strength elastic

Anytime anyplace anywhere
But bathrooms are a no no
Coz the toilet seat has teeth – OW!
And then it's time to go so . . .

IS IT A BIRD?
IS IT A PLANE?
LOOK AT THE SIZE OF THE NOSE ON HIS FACE!
IS IT A BIRD?
IS IT A PLANE?
CAPTAIN CONCORDE IS HIS NAME!
CAPTAIN CONCORDE NEEEEOOWN!
CAPTAIN CONCORDE NEEEEOOWN!

The Amazing Captain Concord . . . he's a superman.
The Amazing Captain Concord . . . super underpants
The Amazing Captain Concord . . . nobody can trick him
The Amazing Captain Concord . . . with a nose like that
    you'd pick him.

Who's the man with the supersonic noise? . . .
Captain Concorde!
Who's the man with horrible taste in clothes? . . .
Captain Concorde!

Who's the man who's always your best friend? . . .
Captain Concorde!
Who's the man who's always set the trend? . . .
Captain Concorde!
Who's the man who's so aerodynamic? . . .
Captain Concorde!
Who's the man who makes the villains panic? . . .
Captain Concorde!
Who's the man who always helps his mum? . . .
Captain Concorde!
Who's the man you'd like to become? . . .
Captain Concorde!
Who? Captain Concorde!
Who? Captain Concorde!
So . . .

IS IT A BIRD?
IS IT A PLANE?
LOOK AT THE SIZE OF THE NOSE ON HIS FACE!
IS IT A BIRD?
IS IT A PLANE?
CAPTAIN CONCORDE IS HIS NAME!
CAPTAIN CONCORDE NEEEEOOWN!
CAPTAIN CONCORDE NEEEEOOWN!

Paul Cookson

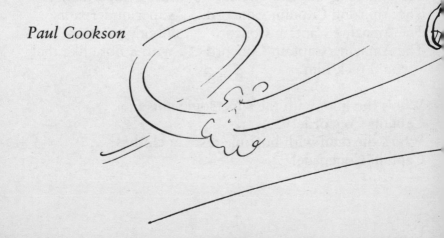

A Fashion Tip for Overweight Superheroes:

Over-
indulging?
Tummy bulging?
Tights tight-fitting?
Side seams splitting?
Out of shape? Buy a cape!

Jane Clarke

Caterpillar Woman

Sometimes she's a butterfly and sometimes she's a pupa;
Sometimes she's a super-spy, a caterpillar snooper;
In the sky she'll flutter by, a super loop-the-looper;
She's tougher than the FBI, a mini-paratrooper.

No matter what the danger, she will never budge or bilk,
Like Spiderman or Superman or others of the ilk.
She ties up all the bad guys with her caterpillar silk
And she lives on leaves of mulberry and aphids' milk.

Caterpillar Woman has a tender heart:
When villains make a run for it they always get a start,
Then she tracks them down and shoots them with her
    holly-prickle darts;
She's tiny and she's fearless and extremely smart.

Caterpillar Woman has a garden shed:
Where she turns into a chrysalis and hangs by her head.
She's got every super comic book you've ever read
And she stacks them up in piles underneath her bed.

Caterpillar Woman has a secret life:
She's an ordinary mother and an ordinary wife,
Makes porridge with a wooden spoon, spreads butter
    with a knife,
Goes shopping every Friday at McNab's in Fyfe.

Caterpillar Women is nobody's fool,
Though she never went to college and she never went
    to school;
She's brilliant at surfing and a champion at pool;
She's green and she's hairy and she's wicked and
    she's cool.

Caterpillar Woman is a one-woman band,
With twenty pairs of trainers and twenty pairs of hands;
She parachutes to safety on a silken strand,
She's the best crime-fighter in the whole of the land.

So listen all you criminals, I'll tell you true:
Be careful what you're thinking and be careful what
    you do,
Give up your naughty habits and start anew
'Cos Caterpillar Woman will be watching out for you!

(Right at this very moment, actually)

Tony Charles

Arthur Wrightus

Don't let those false teeth fool you
don't let that hair loss hide,
the might of Arthur Wrightus
and that walking stick at his side.

He may be seventy-two
he may have lost his teeth,
but inside that cardigan
there's a superhero underneath.

With just one gentle nod
of his old and trusty pipe,
Arthur's one hair stands up
and his long johns go all tight.

His hearing aid starts to crackle
his slippers give off heat
as rockets on his raincoat
fire him from his seat.

And so he's off to save the world
in just a puff of smoke,
for good old Arthur Wrightus
is just that kind of bloke.

Andrew Collett

Superman's Dog

Superman's dog – he's the best
Helping pets in distress
Red and gold pants and vest
'SD' on his chest

Superman's dog – X-ray sight
Green bones filled with Kryptonite
Bright blue lycra tights in flight
Faster than a meteorite

Better than Batman's Robin
Rougher than Robin's bat
Faster than Spiderman's spider
Cooler than Catwoman's cat

Superman's dog – bionic scent
Crime prevention – his intent
Woof and tough – cement he'll dent
What's his name – Bark Kent!

Paul Cookson

The Superhero Training Academy

Timetable for Tuesday

9.30am Leaping tall buildings with a single bound.
Bring crash helmets and permission notes from parents.

10.30am X-ray vision test.
Note: teachers will be wearing lead underwear.

11am Break
No flying in the playground.

11.30am Quick changes into your superclothes.
This lesson will be held at the telephone box by the post office.

12.30pm Lunch
Do remember, after eating your cow pies, do place the horns in the waste bins.
It is extremely dangerous and inconsiderate to leave these things about where people might sit on them.

1.30pm P.E. in our specially re-inforced underground cave. Try not to cause earthquakes with your super exertions.

2.30pm Flying lessons.
Pupils must be wearing capes and tights. Anybody who fails to do this will just have to sit and watch.

3.30pm Hometime
Parents driving Batmobiles are asked once again not to park them on the zig zag lines outside the school gates.

Marian Swinger

Bionic Boy

Faster than a bullet
Stronger than an ox
Bionic Boy cuts quite a dash
In vest and day-glow socks.

Wherever evil threatens good
Bionic Boy will go
'Defender of the Universe'
And all that jazz, you know.

He beats up brutal baddies
He puts them behind bars
He saves the Earth from aliens
From Planet Zog and Mars.

He blasts them with his laser gun
Safe in his flame-proof suit
Then loops-the-loop in victory
Propelled by rocket boots.

Having kept the world from harm
Yet always at the ready
He flies off home to his soft warm bed
And snuggles up to teddy.

Richard Caley

Batgirl's Day Off

Auntie Betty pulls her cloak on
And the mask – the one with ears
Then she goes and does the shopping
In her bashed-up Cavalier.
All the people down Tesco
Bow and curtsey in the aisles
And the queue for autographs
Goes round the block for miles and miles.

But Betty waves them all away
'Sorry. It's my day off today.'

Andrea Shavick